THE *Promise* OF *Heaven*

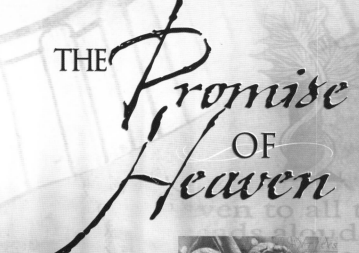

LAHAYE
JENKINS

D1451395

HARVEST HOUSE PUBLISHERS
EUGENE, OREGON

The Promise of Heaven

Copyright © 2003 by Tim LaHaye and Jerry B. Jenkins
Published by Harvest House Publishers
Eugene, Oregon 97402

Library of Congress Cataloging-in-Publication Data

LaHaye, Tim F.
    The promise of heaven / by Tim LaHaye and Jerry B. Jenkins.
        p. cm.
    ISBN 0-7369-1085-9
    1. Heaven--Christianity. 2. God--Promises. 3. Christian life. I.
Jenkins, Jerry B. II. Title.
    BT846.3 .L34 2003
    236'.24--dc21

                                2002011139

Published in association with the literary agency of Alive Communications, Inc.,
7680 Goddard Street, Ste # 200, Colorado Springs, CO 80920.

This book includes excerpts from *Left Behind, Nicolae,* and *Apollyon*. LEFT BEHIND®
trademarks and copyrights are licensed exclusively by Tyndale House Publishers, Carol
Stream, IL. All Rights Reserved.

Prayers are taken from *Perhaps Today*, Copyright © 2001 by Tim LaHaye and
Jerry B. Jenkins. Used by permission of Tyndale House Publishers.

Design and Production by Koechel Peterson & Associates, Inc., Minneapolis, Minnesota

Unless otherwise indicated, all Scripture quotations are taken from the Holy Bible:
New International Version®. NIV®. Copyright © 1973, 1978, 1984 by the International
Bible Society. Used by permission of Zondervan Publishing House. The "NIV" and
"New International Version" trademarks are registered in the United States Patent
and Trademark Office by International Bible Society. Verses marked NKJV are taken
from the New King James Version. Copyright ©1982 by Thomas Nelson, Inc. Used
by permission. All rights reserved. Verses marked KJV are from the King James Version.

Printed in China.

03 04 05 06 07 08 09 10 11 12 / IM / 10 9 8 7 6 5 4 3 2 1

Contents

THE *Promise* OF *Heaven*

by Tim LaHaye and Jerry B. Jenkins

Love

God's love leads to the promise of heaven.

Truth

God's Word made flesh personifies
the truth of our heavenly home.

Faith

With faith, heaven is not an idea
or a possibility—it is a sight to see.

The Gift

The best gift ever given, ever received,
is an eternal home with the Father.

Eternity

When today ends and eternity begins,
heaven will be your dwelling place.

THE *Promise* OF *Heaven*

There is a universal quest in the human heart to live forever, and always the desired location is heaven. The religions of the world have a variety of descriptions for that eternal state, but none is so clear or as descriptive as that given in the Bible.

Mankind's fascination with life after death and the place the Bible calls "heaven" is as old as human history, and even today it is the dream of every normal heart. Jesus Christ, His apostles, and the Hebrew prophets all tapped into that yearning by giving us an incredible array of detail. The Lord Himself, through John, the writer of the book of Revelation, left us two entire chapters on that exotic place.

The loving God who put the quest of heaven in the human heart went to great lengths to make it a sublimely appealing place—there are nearly six hundred references to it in the sixty-six books of His supernaturally revealed Bible. And we should not lose sight of the fact that He started His divine love letter to mankind with two chapters about heaven lost and ended it with two chapters describing heaven found. Adam and Eve lost their heavenly state in the Garden of Eden because of their sin, and consequently they were expelled. Jesus Christ came into this world as God's "only begotten Son" to die sacrificially for that sin and ensure that heaven can yet be gained by those who are willing to believe in Him as their personal Lord and Savior (Romans 10:9-10).

Heaven is still God's ultimate desire for all mankind. Unfortunately, many refuse to accept His Son so they can spend eternity there. We hope this book will inspire you to want to spend your eternity in this most desirable of all places. We hope to meet you there!

TIM LAHAYE and JERRY B. JENKINS

Love

GOD'S LOVE
LEADS TO THE
PROMISE OF HEAVEN.

For God so loved the world that he gave his one and only Son, that whoever believes in him shall not perish but have eternal life. For God did not send his Son into the world to condemn the world, but to save the world through him.

JOHN 3:16–17

It is easy to miss the point of unconditional love. We are too busy looking for the bottom line, searching for "the catch" that will support the human assumption "if it sounds too good to be true…"

But God's love is the real thing. It sounds too good to be true because God's dreams for us are beyond our imagination. The depth of His love and the expanse of heaven—prepared for those who return His love—are beyond units of measure.

Do not compare this love to anything you have ever experienced. This love is strong in its sacrifice, merciful in its comfort, never failing in its presence, and mighty in its pursuit of the heart.

And in our moments of skepticism, when we look for the strings attached, love reveals the heartstrings of heaven.

Irene had always talked of a loving God, but even God's love and mercy had to have limits. Had everyone who denied the truth pushed God to his limit? Was there no more mercy, no second chance? Maybe there wasn't, and if that was so, that was so.

But if there were options, if there was still a way to find the truth and believe or accept or whatever it was Irene said one was supposed to do, Rayford was going to find it. Would it mean admitting that he didn't know everything? That he had relied on himself and that now he felt stupid and weak and worthless? He could admit that. After a lifetime of achieving, of excelling, of being better than most and the best in most circles, he had been as humbled as was possible in one stroke.

"RAYFORD STEELE"
Left Behind

Blessed is the man who perseveres under trial,
because when he has stood the test,
he will receive the crown of life that God
has promised to those who love him.

JAMES 1:12

We love because he first loved us.

1 JOHN 4:19

He made us with the intention that He and we might walk together forever in a love-relationship.... Here, therefore, is a further reason why God speaks to you not only to move us to do what He wants, but to enable us to know Him so that we may love Him. Therefore God sends His word to us in the character of both information and invitation. It comes to woo us as well as to instruct us; it not merely puts us in the picture of what God has done and is doing, but also calls us into personal communion with the loving Lord Himself.

J.I. PACKER

DEAR HEAVENLY FATHER,
Thank You for Your unconditional love! Forgive me when I am unloving. Help me to love like You, beginning today. In Jesus' name I pray, Amen.

No one has ever seen God;

but if we love one another,

God lives in us and his love

is made complete in us.

1 JOHN 4:12

God is to be loved, of course, most of all; heavenly things too are to be much loved...

RICHARD ROLLE

The soul must long for God in order to be set aflame by God's love; but if the soul cannot yet feel this longing, then it must long for the longing. To long for the longing is also from God.

MEISTER ECKHART

LISTEN CLOSELY. *Jesus' love does not depend upon what we do for him. Not at all. In the eyes of the King, you have value simply because you are. You don't have to look nice or perform well. Your value is inborn.*

MAX LUCADO

God demonstrates his own love toward us, in that while we were yet sinners, Christ died for us.

ROMANS 5:8

DEAR HEAVENLY FATHER,
Thank You for Your love and interest in humankind. Thank You for saving me, and please use me to share Your Good News with others. I realize I need Your Holy Spirit to fill my life so I can become a channel of grace to others. In Jesus' name I pray, Amen.

FOR I AM CONVINCED *that neither death nor life,*
neither angels nor demons, neither the present nor the
future, nor any powers, neither height nor depth,
nor anything else in all creation, will be able to separate
us from the love of God that is in Christ Jesus our Lord.

ROMANS 8:38-39

We who live here
in fellowship with him
will one day be with him
in eternal fellowship.

DIETRICH BONHOEFFER

DEAR
HEAVENLY FATHER,
Thank You for the great
plan You have for my
future. I know I don't
deserve such a future,
but I thank You that
it is guaranteed by Your
Word. Please keep this
hope alive in my heart on
a daily basis. Let me live
every moment pleasing
unto You and to Your Son
who loved me and
gave Himself for me.
In Jesus' name I pray,
Amen.

If I speak in the tongues of men and of angels, but have not love, I am only a resounding gong or a clanging cymbal. If I have the gift of prophecy and can fathom all mysteries and all knowledge, and if I have a faith that can move mountains, but have not love, I am nothing. If I give all I possess to the poor and surrender my body to the flames, but have not love, I gain nothing.

Love is patient, love is kind. It does not envy, it does not boast, it is not proud. It is not rude, it is not self-seeking, it is not easily angered, it keeps no record of wrongs. Love does not delight in evil but rejoices with the truth. It always protects, always trusts, always hopes, always perseveres.

1 CORINTHIANS 13:1-7

Those of us who immerse ourselves in God's Word, who press in deeper and deeper, know its power. We love His Word like a love letter we read over and over.

STORMIE OMARTIAN

"For the fruit of the Spirit is in all goodness and righteousness and truth." ~ Ephesians 5:5

truth

GOD'S WORD MADE FLESH
PERSONIFIES THE TRUTH
OF OUR HEAVENLY HOME.

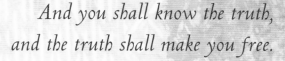

And you shall know the truth,
and the truth shall make you free.

JOHN 8:32, NKJV

Are you attracted to the simplicity of truth?
Or does it startle you with its ability to pare away layers of idle talk,
rote action, and pretense?

When you examine and adopt the truth of Christ's life, such a
"mountaintop experience" can change your outlook. Standing surefooted,
hands on hips, you take in the 360-degree view. With clarity, you survey
all that is important in each of life's valleys and peaks. Absolutes like
compassion, love, and peace rise to the surface of your thoughts,
of your priority list.

From here, trivia does not hinder the view of heaven's glory.
With arms lifted in praise, the wind rushes around, and your soul
understands the psalmist's wish, "Oh, that I had the wings of a dove!
I would fly away and be at rest…"(Psalm 55:6).

This is what it feels like when the simple truth of heaven sets you free.

HOWEVER, WHEN HE, *the spirit of truth,*
has come, he will guide you into all truth;
for he will not speak on his own authority,
but whatever he hears he will speak;
and he will tell you things to come.

JOHN 16:13

They would be on a mission, a quest for truth. If he [Rayford] was already too late, he would have to accept and deal with that. He'd always been one who went for a goal and accepted the consequences. Only these consequences were eternal. He hoped against all hope that there was another chance at truth and knowledge out there somewhere.

"RAYFORD STEELE"
Left Behind

The man who finds a truth lights a torch.

ROBERT G. INGERSOLL

> *Come, and let us go up to the mountain of the LORD,*
>
> *To the house of the God of Jacob;*
>
> *He will teach us His ways,*
>
> *And we shall walk in His paths.*

 MICAH 4:2, NKJV

DEAR LORD,

In this day of deception I want to thank You for those who have carefully
steered me into truth. Thank You for all who had anything to do with my salvation,
and please help me to be a tool in Your hand to teach others the truth
they once taught me. In Your blessed name I pray,

Amen.

I believe it! 'Tis Thou, God,
that givest, 'tis I who receive;
In the first is the last,
in Thy will is my power to believe.
All's one gift; Thou canst grant it moreover,
as prompt my prayer
As I breathe out this breath,
As I open these arms to the air.

ROBERT BROWNING

All of us—even the purest of us—deserve heaven about as much as that crook did. All of us are signing on Jesus' credit card, not ours.

And it also makes me smile to think that there is a grinning ex-con walking the golden streets who knows more about grace than a thousand theologians. No one else would have given him a prayer. But in the end, that is all that he had. And in the end, that is all it took.

MAX LUCADO

I tell you the truth, today you will be with me in paradise.

LUKE 23:43
Jesus, to one of the thieves
crucified beside him.

HE WHO SEES THE TRUTH, *let him proclaim it,*
without asking who is for it or who is against it.
HENRY GEORGE

He is the Rock, His work is perfect;

For all His ways are justice.

A God of truth and without injustice;

Righteous and upright is He.

DEUTERONOMY 32:4, NKJV

> **DEAR LORD,**
> Thank You so much for the comforting truth
> that I again shall one day meet all my loved ones who
> have died in the faith. What other religion can offer such
> life? Please help me to share my faith with others who
> have no such hope because they have not yet received
> You. I want to be used of Your Spirit today.
> In Jesus' name I pray,
> Amen.

"It's really quite simple. God made it easy.

That doesn't mean it's not a supernatural transaction

or that we can pick and choose the good parts—as I tried to do.

But if we see the truth and act on it, God won't withhold salvation from us."

"BRUCE BARNES"
Left Behind

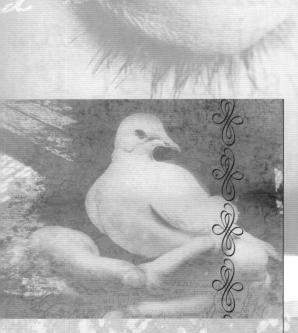

AND THE WORD BECAME *flesh and dwelt among us, and we beheld His glory, the glory as of the only begotten of the Father, full of grace and truth.... No one has seen God at any time. The only begotten Son, who is in the bosom of the Father, He has declared Him.*

JOHN 1:14,18, NKJV

Our Lord has written
the promise of the resurrection
not in books alone,
but in every leaf in springtime.

MARTIN LUTHER

Christ is the truth about God, the life of God, and the way to God. The more we know of Christ, the more we know of God....We will know the truth, and living it will set us free. Humbly we can say we know God. Truth and mercy will be the mark of our integrity. Nothing is more important.

LLOYD JOHN OGILVIE

Sanctify them by Your truth.
Your word is truth.

JOHN 17:17, NKJV

All Rayford could do was pray. "Lord," he said silently, "I wish I was a more willing servant. Is there no other role for me?... I can only trust in your purpose. Keep my loved ones safe until we see you in all your glory. I know you have long since forgiven me for my years of disbelief and indifference, but still it weighs heavily on me. Thank you for helping me find the truth..."

"RAYFORD STEELE"
Nicolae

But he who does the truth comes to the light,
that his deeds may be clearly seen,
that they have been done in God.

JOHN 3:21

Faith

WITH FAITH, HEAVEN
IS NOT AN IDEA OR A POSSIBILITY—
IT IS A SIGHT TO SEE.

No eye has seen, no ear has heard, no mind has conceived
what God has prepared for those who love him.

Many say that faith is believing in something you cannot see.
But when we have faith, we witness the fruit of this faith in our lives.
Forgiveness. Love. Righteousness.

When we are hungry or thirsty, we cannot see the force within us,
but it carries us toward fulfillment. So it is with faith. We are pulled
along by an unseen desire to be led, fulfilled, and tethered to heaven by
God. Our eyes open to the blessings of a relationship with the Lord. We
turn to Scripture to view models of servanthood. And we
witness God's faithfulness to His children daily.

There is much to see when one has faith.
The promises of heaven are revealed. And this time, seeing is believing.

For in the gospel,

a righteousness from God is revealed,

a righteousness that is by faith

from first to last, just as it is written:

"The righteous will live by faith."

ROMANS 1:17

The only Bible verse Rayford could quote by heart was Genesis 1:1: "In the beginning God created the heavens and the earth." He hoped there'd be some corresponding verse at the end of the Bible that said something like, "In the end God took all his people to heaven and gave everybody else one more chance."

But no such luck. The very last verse in the Bible meant nothing to him. It said, "The grace of the Lord Jesus be with you all. Amen." And it sounded like the religious mumbo jumbo he had heard in church. He backed up a verse and read, "He who testifies to these things says, 'Yes, I am coming quickly.' Amen. Come, Lord Jesus."

…But near the end of the chapter was a verse that ended with words that had a strange impact on him. Without a hint of their meaning, he read, "Let the one who is thirsty come; let the one who wishes take the water of life without cost."…It struck him that he was thirsty, soul thirsty.

"RAYFORD STEELE"
Left Behind

WHATEVER WE DO, *it is because Christ's love controls us. Since we believe that Christ died for everyone, we also believe that we have all died to the old life we used to live. He died for everyone so that those who receive his new life will no longer live to please themselves. Instead, they will live to please Christ, who died and was raised for them.*

2 CORINTHIANS 5:14-15

DEAR HEAVENLY FATHER,
Forgive me for the times that I have let the cares of my life "trouble" my heart. I know You have been there for me all the time, and I sin when I fail to trust You. Please increase my faith, then help me to allow my faith to quiet my troubled heart. In Jesus' name I pray, Amen.

There is only one being who can satisfy the last aching abyss of the human heart, and that is the Lord Jesus Christ.

OSWALD CHAMBERS

THEREFORE, *since we have been justified through faith, we have peace with God through our Lord Jesus Christ, through whom we have gained access by faith into this grace in which we now stand. And we rejoice in the hope of the glory of God. Not only so, but we also rejoice in our sufferings, because we know that suffering produces perseverance; perseverance, character; and character, hope. And hope does not disappoint us, because God has poured out his love into our hearts by the Holy Spirit, whom he has given us.*

ROMANS 5:1-5

Through the dark and stormy night

Faith beholds a feeble light

Up the blackness streaking

Knowing God's own time is best

In a patient hope I rest

For the full day-breaking!

JOHN GREENLEAF WHITTIER

*Prayer is the key to heaven,
but faith unlocks the door.*

KAY ARTHUR

By nature God is a self-revealer; he must make himself known. Yet God is a self-concealer as well. "The secret things belong to the Lord our God," Moses told the Israelites. We live dangling between the secret things, withheld perhaps for our own protection, and the revealed things. The God who satisfies our thirst is also the great Unknown, the one no one can look upon and live. Perhaps it takes God's absence and presence both for us to remain ourselves, or even to survive.

PHILIP YANCEY
Reaching for the Invisible God

But without faith it is impossible to please Him,
for he who comes to God must believe that He is,
and that He is a rewarder of those who diligently seek Him.

HEBREWS 11:6, NKJV

DEAR HEAVENLY FATHER, Thank You for Your encouraging promise. Give us joy in Your pledge that You are literally coming again to take us to Your house, which Your Son even now prepares. May we be found faithful in serving You as long as we have life. And for today, lead us to make all our decisions in the light of Jesus' coming. Further, make us so sensitive to Your leading that we, in joy, reach out to share the promise with others. In Jesus' name, Amen.

In him and through faith in him we may approach God with freedom and confidence.
EPHESIANS 3:12-13

We know indeed that seeking is never without its promise, how then could we fail to seek You, the author of all promises and the giver of all good gifts!
SOREN KIERKEGAARD

Praise be to the God and Father of our Lord Jesus Christ! In his great mercy he has given us new birth into a living hope through the resurrection of Jesus Christ from the dead, and into an inheritance that can never perish, spoil or fade—kept in heaven for you, who through faith are shielded by God's power until the coming of the salvation that is ready to be revealed in the last time.

1 PETER 1:3-5

DEAR LORD,
We are humbled at the way You reach out to us and encourage our faith. There are times in our lives when we become weak in the faith. Your second coming has already taken a long, long time. But Your Word and its fulfillment gives us the faith to keep on trusting and serving You....
In Jesus' name, Amen.

THE *Gift*

THE BEST GIFT EVER GIVEN,
EVER RECEIVED, IS AN ETERNAL
HOME WITH THE FATHER.

In my Father's house are many rooms; if it were not so, I would have told you. I am going there to prepare a place for you. And if I go and prepare a place for you, I will come back and take you to be with me that you also may be where I am. You know the way to the place where I am going.

JOHN 14:1-4

"Do not open until Christmas." As a child, did you ever receive a gift with this condition scrawled on the tag or outer wrapping? You would hold, shake, and scrutinize the package while eating Thanksgiving leftovers and wonder how Aunt Sylvia or Uncle Howard could be so unreasonable.

Our heavenly Father understands that great anticipation. In fact, He created it in each of us so that when the time came for His Son to die on the cross and rise three days later, we would immediately recognize Calvary for what it was. The best gift *ever*.

And upon recognizing this gift, you can ignore the "conditions" scrawled on your heart by years of doubt, failure, or pain…and *open* it. Embrace it. Share it with everyone you meet.

And as you do, your name will be known throughout heaven, for a place is being prepared for you…with your name on it. And the card reads, "Already opened at Easter."

Have mercy on me, O God, according to your unfailing love; according to your great compassion blot out my transgressions. Wash away all my iniquity and cleanse me from my sin....Create in me a pure heart, O God, and renew a steadfast spirit within me. Do not cast me from your presence or take your Holy Spirit from me. Restore to me the joy of your salvation and grant me a willing spirit, to sustain me.

PSALM 51: 1–2, 11–12

He knew he needed Christ in his life. He needed forgiveness of sin and the assurance that one day he would join his wife and son in heaven....Rayford sat with his head in his hands, his heart pounding. There was no sound from upstairs where Chloe rested. He was alone with his thoughts, alone with God, and he felt God's presence. Rayford slid to his knees on the carpet. He had never knelt in worship before, but he sensed the seriousness and the reverence of the moment....He set his hands palms down before him and rested his forehead on them, his face on the floor.

The pastor said, "Pray after me," and Rayford did. "Dear God, I admit that I'm a sinner. I am sorry for my sins. Please forgive me and save me. I ask this in the name of Jesus, who died for me. I trust in him right now. I believe that the sinless blood of Jesus is sufficient to pay the price for my salvation. Thank you for hearing me and receiving me. Thank you for saving my soul."

RAYFORD STEELE'S PRAYER OF SALVATION
Left Behind

DEAR LORD,

Thank You for making me a citizen of heaven freely by Your grace. I do not deserve this privilege, but I thank You for it. I sincerely desire to live each day in conformity to Your will. Help me to avoid earthly minded decisions and "set [my] affection on things above." May I commit all my ways to You. Use my life as You see fit. In Jesus' name,

Amen.

Bring us, O Lord God, at our last awakening, into the house and gate of heaven, to enter into that gate and dwell in that house where there shall be no darkness nor dazzling, but one equal light; no noise nor silence, but one equal music; no fears nor hopes, but one equal possession; no ends nor beginnings, but one equal eternity; in the habitations of Thy glory and dominion, world without end. Amen.

JOHN DONNE

For our citizenship is in heaven, from which we also eagerly wait for the Savior, the Lord Jesus Christ, who will transform our lowly body that it may be conformed to His glorious body, according to the working by which He is able even to subdue all things to Himself. Therefore, my beloved and longed-for brethren, my joy and crown, so stand fast in the Lord, beloved.

PHILIPPIANS 3:20–4:1, NKJV

Now may the God of peace Himself sanctify you completely; and may your whole spirit, soul, and body be preserved blameless at the coming of our Lord Jesus Christ.

1 THESSALONIANS 5:23, NKJV

"I see now, of course, that God is a sin-forgiving God, because we're human and we need that. But we are to receive his gift, abide in Christ, and allow him to live through us"

"BRUCE BARNES"
Left Behind

Lord, make me an instrument of Your peace; where there is hatred, let me sow love; where there is injury, pardon; where there is doubt, faith; where there is despair, hope; where there is darkness, light; and where there is sadness, joy.

O Divine Master, grant that I may not so much seek to be consoled as to console; to be understood, as to understand; to be loved as to love. For it is in giving that we receive, it is in pardoning that we are pardoned, and it is in dying that we are born to eternal life.

FRANCIS OF ASSISI

DEAR HEAVENLY FATHER,

I thank You that You have a specific will for my life. I may not fully
understand what that will is, but I have faith in Your love for me….
From now until Jesus comes for me, I want to be under Your direction.
I give myself totally to You. In Jesus' name I pray,

Amen.

The gift of eternal life is there to be received. So take God's gift while you still have time…. There's a time to reject and a time to accept. Make this your time to accept.

CHARLES R. SWINDOLL

As if he had heard Jacov, Tsion repeated the verse: "'For God so loved the world that He gave His only begotten Son, that whoever believes in Him should not perish but have everlasting life.'"

Jacov lowered his face to the pavement, sobbing. "I believe! I believe! God save me! Don't let me perish! Give me everlasting life!"

"He hears you," Buck said. "He will not turn away a true seeker."

But Jacov continued to wail. Others in the crowd had fallen to their knees. Tsion said, "There may be some here, inside or outside, who want to receive Christ. I urge you to pray after me, 'Dear God, I know I am a sinner. Forgive me and pardon me for waiting so long. I receive your love and salvation and ask you to live your life through me. I accept you as my Savior and resolve to live for you until you come again.'"

Apollyon

See how very much our heavenly Father loves us, for he allows us to be called his children, and we really are! But the people who belong to this world don't know God, so they don't understand that we are his children. Yes, dear friends, we are already God's children, and we can't even imagine what we will be like when Christ returns. But we do know that when he comes we will be like him, for we will see him as he really is. And all who believe this will keep themselves pure, just as Christ is pure.

1 JOHN 31:11-5, NKJV

DEAR HEAVENLY FATHER,
I stand in awe before the wonder of Your salvation. Thank You for saving me and forgiving my sins. Because of Your grace and faithfulness, I realize that all my sin is now under the blood. Please help me to leave the punishment of those who have persecuted me to You, praying that they will receive Your grace and forgiveness even as I have. Help me to forgive them for whatever they have done against me. I want to be pure and free from all grudges at the coming of Jesus.
In His name I pray,
Amen.

What we have been told is how we can be drawn into Christ—can become part of that wonderful present which the young Prince of the universe wants to offer his Father—that present which is Himself and therefore us in Him. It is the only thing we were made for.

C.S. LEWIS

GOD RAISED *him up to the heights of heaven and gave him a name that is above every other name, so that at the name of Jesus every knee will bow, in heaven and on earth and under the earth, and every tongue will confess that Jesus Christ is Lord to the glory of God the Father.*

PHILIPPIANS 2:9-11

O Father of eternal life, and all
Created glories under thee!
Resume thy spirit from this world of thrall
Into true liberty.

HENRY VAUGHAN

Now we have received, not the spirit
of the world, but the Spirit who is from God,
that we might know the things that have been
freely given to us by God. These things we
also speak not in words which man's wisdom
teaches but which the Holy Spirit teaches,
comparing spiritual things with spiritual.

1 CORINTHIANS 2:12-13

Eternity

WHEN TODAY ENDS
AND ETERNITY BEGINS,
HEAVEN WILL BE
YOUR DWELLING PLACE
WITH THE LORD.

These things I have written to you who believe in the name of the Son of God, that you may know that you have eternal life, and that you may continue to believe in the name of the Son of God.

1 JOHN 5:13, NKJV

We have planners, computers, and personal assistants to schedule our earthly days. We tout the benefits of living in a society where we can get anything at a moment's notice. We live one day at a time but often orchestrate those days with agonizing precision.

Yet, how often do we pay attention to matters of eternity? There are no software programs that schedule the days to be spent with the Lord, but an eternal plan is written on your heart and your soul.

Have you given your "forever" the attention that you should? The One who made time and created your today wants to spend eternity with you.

All the days ordained for me
were written in your book
before one of them came to be.

PSALM 31:15

Teach me, Lord, to sing of Your mercies. Turn my soul into a garden, where the flowers dance in the gentle breeze, praising You with their beauty. Let my soul be filled with beautiful virtues; let me be inspired by Your Holy Spirit; let me praise You always.

TERESA OF AVILA

"God, fill me with courage, with power, with whatever I need to be a witness. I don't want to be afraid anymore. I don't want to wait any longer. I don't want to worry about offending. Give me a persuasiveness rooted in the truth of your Word. I know it is your Spirit that draws people, but use me. I want to reach Chloe. I want to reach Hattie. Please, Lord. Help me."

RAYFORD STEELE'S PRAYER
Left Behind

If our faith is firmly fixed in the Savior, we can count on Him to be waiting at the end of the road to greet us. In fact, He'll be waiting up for us. Our room is ready. The light is on. We are expected. He will welcome us home.

CHARLES R. SWINDOLL

DEAR HEAVENLY FATHER,
Thank You for sending Jesus Your Son into this world to die for my sins and the sins of the whole world. Thank You for His wonderful promise to take us up to Your house to be with Him, Amen.

They were longing for a better country—a heavenly one. Therefore God is not ashamed to be called their God, for he has prepared a city for them.

HEBREWS 11:16

NOW WE KNOW *that if the earthly tent we live in is destroyed, we have a building from God, an eternal house in heaven, not built by human hands.*

2 CORINTHIANS 5:1

Your soul has a curious shape because it is a hollow made to fit a particular swelling in the infinite contours of the divine substance, or a key to unlock one of the doors in the house with many mansions. For it is not humanity in the abstract that is to be saved, but you—you the individual reader...Blessed and fortunate creature, your eyes shall behold Him and not another's. All that you are, sins apart, is destined, if you let God have His good way, to utter satisfaction....Your place in Heaven will seem to be made for you and you alone, because you were made for it.

C.S. LEWIS

All the ends of the world shall remember and turn to the LORD
and all the families of the nations shall worship before You.

PSALM 22:27, NKJV

My soul, there is a country

Far beyond the stars,

Where stands a winged sentry

All skillful in the wars;

There above noise, and danger,

Sweet Peace sits crowned with smiles,

And One born in a manger

Commands the beauteous files.

HENRY VAUGHAN

DEAR LORD,
It is so easy for me to take my eyes from the promises of Jesus' coming. Many times I spend too much of my time thinking of this world and all of its cares. Help me to maintain an eternal perspective and do what is necessary for my family. But never let me forget that heaven is my real home. Help me to so live that when I arrive there, I will have taken many with me. Use my life today. In Jesus' name, Amen.

Then, crowned again, their golden harps they took.

Harps ever tuned, that glittering by their side

Like quivers hung, and with preamble sweet

Of charming symphony they introduce

Their sacred song, and waken raptures high;

No voice exempt, no voice but well could join

Melodious part, such concord is in heaven.

JOHN MILTON

And he will send forth his angels with the
sound of a mighty trumpet blast, and they
will gather together his chosen ones from the
farthest ends of the earth and heaven.

MATTHEW 24:31

For the Lord Himself will
descend from heaven with a shout,
with the voice of an archangel,
and with the trumpet of God.

1 THESSALONIANS 4:16, NKJV

*And this is eternal life,
that they may know You,
the only true God,
and Jesus Christ whom
You have sent.*

JOHN 17:3, NKJV

*For assuredly, I say to you,
till heaven and earth pass away,
one jot or one tittle will by no means
pass from the law till all is fulfilled.*

MATTHEW 5:18, NKJV

But none of these things move me;
nor do I count my life dear to myself,
so that I may finish my race with
joy, and the ministry which I received
from the Lord Jesus, to testify
to the gospel of the grace of God.

ACTS 20:24, NKJV

The end we ought to propose to
ourselves is to become, in this life,
the most perfect worshipers of God
we can possibly be, as we hope to be
through all eternity.

BROTHER LAWRENCE

AND I HEARD *a great voice out of heaven saying, Behold, the tabernacle of God is with men, and he will dwell with them, and they shall be his people, and God himself shall be with them, and be their God.*

REVELATION 21:1-3, KJV

There, also, we shall meet thousands and thousands that have gone before us to that place; none of them hurtful, but loving and holy, everyone walking in the sight of God, and standing in his presence with acceptance forever.

JOHN BUNYAN
The Pilgrim's Progress

Jesus said to him, "It is as you said. Nevertheless, I say to you, hereafter you will see the Son of Man sitting at the right hand of the Power, and coming on the clouds of heaven."

MATTHEW 26:64, NKJV

"Ask anyone on the street what they think the Bible or the church says about getting to heaven, and nine of ten would say it has something to do with doing good and living right.

"We're to do that, of course, but not so we can earn our salvation. We're to do that in response to our salvation. The Bible says that it's not by works of righteousness that we have done, but by his mercy God saved us. It also says that we are saved by grace through Christ, not of ourselves, so we can't brag about our goodness.

"Jesus took our sins and paid the penalty for them so we wouldn't have to. The payment is death, and he died in our place because he loved us. When we tell Christ that we acknowledge ourselves as sinners and lost, and receive his gift of salvation, he saves us. A transaction takes place. We go from darkness to light, from lost to found; we're saved."

"BRUCE BARNES"
Left Behind